GET INVOLVED!

SOCIAL JUSTICE ACTIVIST

STOP EXECUTIONS!
MARIANIST SOC-JUSTICE COLLABORATIVE

NO DEATH PENALTY

Ellen Rodger and
Jon Eben Field

Be a Junior Activist
BIG MOUTH

Crabtree Publishing Company
www.crabtreebooks.com

W9-AXP-322

Crabtree Publishing Company

www.crabtreebooks.com

For today's activists, who need to know and remember the past in order to make a better tomorrow.

Developed and produced by Plan B Book Packagers

Authors:
Ellen Rodger
Jon Eben Field

Art director:
Rosie Gowsell-Pattison

Editor:
Carrie Gleason

Researcher:
Jessie Rodger

Production Coordinator:
Margaret Amy Salter

Crabtree Editor:
Molly Aloian

Crabtree Proofreader:
Kathy Middleton

Photographs:
Associated Press: front cover
Corbis: Jon Hrusa/epa: p. 26; Lynn Goldsmith: p. 27

iStockPhoto: p. 16, 17
Shutterstock: luminouslens: cover (paper); Robert J. Daveant: p. 1; Morgan Rauscher: p. 4, 9; Kuzma: p. 5 (top); Vladimir Melnik: p. 5 (bottom); Christina Richards: p. 6, 22 (bottom right); John Kershner: p. 7; Peter S.: p. 8; Rorem: p. 10; Ken Durden: p. 11; Birute Vijeikiene: p. 12; Provasilich: p. 13; Mandy Godbehear: p. 14; WilleeCole: p. 15; JustASC: p. 18; ImageDesign: p. 19; Ariadna de Raadt: p. 20; Vospalej: p. 21 (top); Caleb Foster: p. 21 (bottom); Karla Caspari: p. 22 (bottom left); Petr Meshkov: p. 23 (top); zeber: p. 23 (bottom); Pakhnyushcha: p. 24 (right); Ivelin Radkov: p. 24 (left); Yury Asotov: p. 25; Kojoku: p. 28; Losevsky Pavel: p. 29 (top); Crystal Kirk: p. 31

Cover: Children in Hyderabad, India, wear masks and participate in an awareness run to mark World Day against Child Labor on June 12, 2008.

Title page: A social justice volunteer group protests the death penalty.

Field Notes credits: page 15, Ali Bandiare quotation from a speech delivered at the World Conference Against Racism, Racial Discrimination, Xenophobia and Related Intolerance, and courtesy of the International Federation of Red Cross and Red Crescent Societies.

Publisher's note to teachers and parents
Although careful consideration has been made in selecting the list of Web sites, due to the nature of the subjects' content some Web sites may contain or have a link to content and images of a sensitive nature. The views and opinions presented in these Web sites are those of the organization and do not represent the views and policies of Crabtree Publishing. As Web site content and addresses often change, Crabtree Publishing accepts no liability for the content of the Web sites.

Library and Archives Canada Cataloguing in Publication

Rodger, Ellen
    Social justice activist / Ellen Rodger and Jon Eben Field.

(Get involved!)
Includes index.
ISBN 978-0-7787-4696-6 (bound).--ISBN 978-0-7787-4708-6 (pbk.).

    1. Social reformers--Juvenile literature. 2. Social justice--Juvenile literature. 3. Social action--Juvenile literature. I. Field, Jon Eben, 1975-
II. Title. III. Series: Get involved!

HM671.R63 2010   j303.3'72   C2009-902425-X

Library of Congress Cataloging-in-Publication Data

Rodger, Ellen.
    Social justice activist / Ellen Rodger and Jon Eben Field.
        p. cm. -- (Get involved!)
    Includes index.
    ISBN 978-0-7787-4708-6 (pbk. : alk. paper) -- ISBN 978-0-7787-4696-6
(reinforced library binding : alk. paper)
    1. Social justice--Juvenile literature. 2. Social action--Juvenile literature. I. Field,
Jon Eben. II. Title. III. Series.

HM671.R65 2010
303.3'72--dc22

2009016725

Crabtree Publishing Company

www.crabtreebooks.com   1-800-387-7650

Published in Canada
Crabtree Publishing
616 Welland Ave.
St. Catharines, ON
L2M 5V6

Published in the United States
Crabtree Publishing
PMB16A
350 Fifth Ave., Suite 3308
New York, NY 10118

Published in the United Kingdom
Crabtree Publishing
White Cross Mills
High Town, Lancaster
LA1 4XS

Published in Australia
Crabtree Publishing
386 Mt. Alexander Rd.
Ascot Vale (Melbourne)
VIC 3032

Contents

GET INVOLVED!

What is social justice?

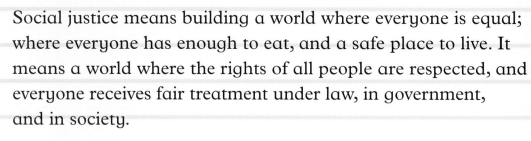

Social justice means building a world where everyone is equal; where everyone has enough to eat, and a safe place to live. It means a world where the rights of all people are respected, and everyone receives fair treatment under law, in government, and in society.

What is just?

Does the thought of millions of people struggling to find enough to eat disturb you? Do you see homeless people on the street and think about how they got there? Have you ever wondered what you can do to stop racism, work for peace, and make the planet a better place for all? If so, then social justice activism is something you might want to investigate.

Activists' work

Social justice activists believe that one person acting alone can make things better, but if we all act together we can change the world. Social justice includes many different issues. Most activists devote their time to one or two causes. Some are **advocates** for people's rights to clean water, education, or **democracy**. Others donate money or time to groups that try to end poverty, improve education, or fight for the rights of women and other **oppressed** groups.

Social justice activists believe that they must help others and that the struggles of people in different countries and social groups affects us all.

Social justice activists believe that everyone has the right to safe and secure housing. They work to help prevent homelessness.

Get Active!

BIG MOUTH

Put yourself in someone else's shoes

Watch the news tonight or read a newspaper. Put yourself in someone else's shoes. Think about how it would feel if you were forced to suddenly flee your home because of war. You might not have anything except the clothes on your back and you could be separated from your parents or other family members. Write your feelings down in a notebook: How would it feel to be afraid of bombs or bullets? Does it make you feel differently about the suffering of other people?

The remains of a bombed-out apartment building in Grozny, Chechen Republic. For safety, the building's residents moved to refugee camps during the republic's war with Russia.

What is an activist?

Activists are people who want to make change. They educate, **agitate**, and offer assistance. Social justice activists believe in equality and justice, and they work to make the world a better and more fair place.

What do they do?

Activists do many things. Some activists are researchers who study world issues and events and publish their findings. They educate and let the world know about social injustices. Others use **grassroots** activities such as public speeches, marches, and presentations to encourage change. Social justice activists also volunteer their time to help people. Some volunteer at local homeless shelters, at school breakfast or sports programs, and at places of worship that promote social justice causes. Others travel far away to work for **humanitarian agencies** that help people in other countries.

Students take part in an anti-war protest. Protests like this are called "direct action." Activists do more than just protest, they also educate and try to change people's attitudes.

Actions and words

Social justice activists believe in the power of both words and actions. Writing letters to politicians and business leaders asking them to help change laws can be as important as marching in a protest. Activists also raise funds, join or form groups, and learn as much as they can about an issue. Most importantly, they refuse to be intimidated, or frightened into abandoning their beliefs by others who do not believe in the same things.

Field Notes:

Using strikes and boycotts as a means of protest, César Chávez fought for the rights of farm workers such as this California grape picker.

César Chávez (1923-1993) was a Mexican-American farm worker and activist who co-founded the National Farm Workers Association, later the United Farm Workers. Early in his career, Chávez was a community organizer who supported farm workers and encouraged Mexican Americans to vote. With the United Farm Workers, Chávez organized strikes and boycotts for better wages and working conditions.

"Once social change begins it can not be reversed. You cannot un-educate the person that has learned to read. You cannot humiliate the person who feels pride. You cannot oppress the people who are not afraid anymore"

Voters line up outside a Chicago polling station to cast their ballots. Voting is one right that citizens have in "free," or democratic countries. Organizing and protesting as an activist is another.

A just society

An image of Dr. Martin Luther King Jr., a U.S. civil rights leader who fought for equality in the 1950s and 60s.

Social justice tries to ensure that we live in a fair, or "just," society. A just society is where the rights of all humans are respected.

Social justice and human rights

Human rights are the basic rights to which all people are **entitled**. They must constantly be protected. Social justice goes further and addresses the questions of what is right and how to make things just. Is it right that some people live in severe poverty in the same city where others have more than enough? Is it right that in many areas of the world, women and girls are not considered as important as men and boys? Is it fair and just that some people do not have access to clean drinking water or the medical care they need to survive?

 **Get Active!** **Choosing your words**

By changing the words that you use every day, you can make a strong stand for social justice. You can speak up for people whose rights are being ignored by refusing to use words or laugh at jokes that are hurtful or racist. This might seem like a small and insignificant action, but the impact of changing your language is important. If someone around you uses a word that insults a person or group of people, it is important to speak up! Let them know that their words are hurtful not only to their target but to everyone's right to be free of prejudice.

Minorities belong to racial or political groups with fewer members than the rest of society. In a just society, people unite and fight for everyone's rights.

Why just?

You might ask yourself why you need to live in a just society. If you do not protect others from human rights abuses, who will care when your human rights are **violated**? If you do not care about the homeless, why would anyone care about you if you lost your home? But social justice activism is not only about self-interest, or caring about others because you may need someone to care about you. It is also about doing what is **ethical**.

Caring for others

To live in a just society, we need to be concerned about each and every person who lives in our community. If it becomes easy for more **vulnerable** members of society to have their rights violated, what's stopping our rights from also being disregarded?

Truth and rights

Human rights include political rights such as the right to life, liberty, and the right to vote or voice an opinion. They also include social, cultural, or economic rights such as the right to food, education, and work.

For everyone

Human rights belong to everyone regardless of race, **gender**, religion, political beliefs, or age. Many countries have human rights laws, **civil rights** laws, or charters. On an international level, the **United Nations** has a Universal Declaration of Human Rights that many countries have signed. These laws and declarations must be enforced to be useful. Often, it is activists who bring attention to human rights abuses and fight against them.

Get Active!   Resistance is not futile

Scholar Margaret Mead once said, "never doubt that a small group of thoughtful, committed citizens can change the world. Indeed it is the only thing that ever has." Her words are important for young activists. Fighting for something you believe in requires commitment. It requires you to resist things that are wrong, even if others think it is silly. Social justice activists often use passive resistance, such as refusing to buy a product made in an unjust manner. Passive resistance means refusing to comply, cooperate, or go along with something you think is wrong. Sometimes it is the safest way to protest. Do some research on passive resistance to see how it has been used. Can you think of a reason to use passive resistance today?

Steady pressure

Every Thursday for the past 30 years, a group of women has marched at a city square in Buenos Aires, Argentina. The Mothers of the Plaza De Mayo are dedicated to finding out what happened to their children and grandchildren who disappeared during Argentina's Dirty War, a period of **repression** that took place from 1976 to 1983. Thousands of people were arrested, tortured, and killed by the country's military government. Their families never knew what happened to them. The Mothers of the Plaza De Mayo are social justice activists who have become symbols of courage and endurance. Some have even been killed in their quest to force the government to tell the truth about what happened to their children.

The Mothers of the Plaza De Mayo wear white kerchiefs on their heads and often carry signs with photographs of their children. The mothers claim "the only struggle you lose is the one you abandon."

Fighting inequality

The fight for equality is one of the cornerstones, or foundations, of social justice. Equality means being equal in rights, opportunities, and social and economic status. Social justice activists believe all people should also have the same opportunities or access to education, law, and the goods and resources of the world.

What is fair?

Sometimes people say: the world isn't fair, that's just how it is. Social justice activists do not accept that nothing can be done. They do what they can to make things fair. They believe **social inequality** is something that can be changed by:

- Ensuring human rights are respected everywhere.
- Pushing for laws and policies that promote equality, such as state-sponsored education for all children.
- Changing attitudes toward inequality, especially the idea that people deserve to be poor because of who they are or where they live.

By choosing to act ethically, and treat people fairly, you can make a big difference in the fight against inequality.

Over 100 million children worldwide do not attend school because they cannot afford to, or must work or care for their brothers and sisters.

Fight inequality by buying certified fair trade products. Fair trade promotes paying a fair price for products. The money paid for these fair trade bananas goes to the farmer, not a company, to give him or her a better standard of living.

Who benefits from inequality?

Inequality is unfair because people are treated differently in ways that are often based on prejudice. It is also unfair that a group or person benefits from inequality or uses their power to create an inequality.

Get Active! Inequality and the G8

The G8 summit is a yearly meeting of leaders of eight of the most powerful nations in the world. They discuss trade and economics. Many activists believe the G8 could help fight inequality in the world, if it wanted to. At each G8 summit, demonstrations are held to convince politicians that people are suffering from G8 economic decisions such as trade restrictions on developing countries. Sometimes the demonstrators are turned back by riot police with tear gas. The inequality that the G8 protesters focus on is worldwide, but making things equal starts with small acts. Think of ways you can change an unequal situation in your community. Research the situation, ask questions, and keep notes. Start a letter-writing campaign or gather with a group of people who feel the same way, and create a movement. Recognizing that an injustice is real and agreeing on a course of action is one of the first steps to activism.

Gender inequality

Every year on March 8, women around the world gather for International Women's Day (IWD). They hold marches, rallies, and concerts to press for equality. The first IWD was marked in 1909. Since then, women in most countries have gained the right to vote, yet they are still unequal in pay and status in many places.

Why equality?

Seventy percent of the world's 1.2 billion people who live in poverty are women. Throughout the world, women raise and support families, but poverty and traditional views about the roles of women often prevent them from being educated. Denied education, they cannot make enough money to escape poverty.

A long way...

Despite many gains in the last 100 years, women all over the world are still striving for equality. Women's rights activists combat inequality by pressing for equality in laws, wages, and education, opposing violence against women, and running shelters for abused women. In many areas of the world, women's rights activists risk their lives just by voicing their opinions. In Iran, women's rights activists organized a One Million Signatures campaign to change gender descrimination in Iranian laws. Several activists were held in jail and questioned. Others were convicted for holding previous demonstrations and sentenced to up to three years in jail.

A marcher in a Women's Day parade dresses in chains as a sympbol of the status of many women in the world.

Susan B. Anthony (1820-1906) was an organizer for the women's movement in the United States. An active speaker and **suffragette**, she used her sharp intelligence to point out gender inequality. One of her moving speeches from 1873 used the U.S. Constitution to fight for the right to vote. Women gained the right to vote in the U.S. in 1920. Anthony's speech begins:

"It was we, the people; not we, the white male citizens; nor yet we, the male citizens; but we, the whole people, who formed the Union. And we formed it, not to give the blessings of liberty, but to secure them; not to the half of ourselves and the half of our posterity, but to the whole people – women as well as men. And it is a downright mockery to talk to women of their enjoyment of the blessings of liberty while they are denied the use of the only means of securing them provided by this democratic-republican government—the ballot. "

Susan B. Anthony was honored as the first woman to appear on a U.S. dollar coin in 1978.

Fighting racism

Racism is a form of discrimination based on the belief that some races are superior to others. Racism **devalues** people because of their skin color or ethnic background. Many racist beliefs are based on stereotypes, which are inaccurate and false views of people.

Hidden or open

Racism can be overt, such as using slurs or being prejudiced. It can also be subtle or partially hidden, like when someone outwardly pretends not to believe in stereotypes but secretly does. Racism can also be systemic or institutional. This means that people of color or certain ethnic backgrounds have less privilege in schools, government, or business. Racism that is part of a system is difficult to fight because people often deny it exists.

Racism and social justice

Social justice activists have been fighting racism for a long time. They do this by embracing the differences in individuals and cultures, and by working actively against prejudice. Tactics used to battle racism include: uniting in anti-racist groups, speaking up against and exposing prejudice, and learning about **diversity** through understanding other cultures.

Societies that accept and celebrate cultural diversity are often better at fighting racism. Cultural diversity means that people have a variety of different backgrounds and cultures.

Field Notes:

Ali Bandiare, Vice President of the International Federation of Red Cross and Red Crescent Societies, delivered a speech at a world anti-racism conference in 2001. The Red Cross and Red Crescent Societies are humanitarian organizations that help victims of disasters, wars, and violence. Also the President of the Red Cross Society in the African country of Niger, Bandiare said it takes volunteers, especially youth, to wipe out ideas that support racism. Here is a part of his speech:

"Racism is not only a shameful page in our history. It is not entirely behind us. Outdated ideas and antiquated mindsets are still present and accepted. Discriminatory laws and practices are very much in vigor in some places. In other places, people accept, silently, the more subtle forms of discrimination. Those hidden practices, that no-one will admit exists, that make it more difficult for some people than others to obtain justice, fair representation, access to the labor or housing market, or even a visa. Racism and racial discrimination make a mockery out of human dignity. No rhetoric about equality and fairness is credible if we accept racism and racial discrimination."

STOP

Fighting poverty

Poverty means living without – without enough **nutritious** food, proper shelter, or clothing to keep you warm or dry. Poverty is a social justice issue in developed, or wealthy, areas of the world as well as in the **developing world**.

People in a developing country pick through garbage, looking for food and items to sell.

Measuring poverty

In the developing world, poverty is measured by how much money a person spends to live. An estimated 1.4 billion people in poorer countries (one in four people) live on less than $1.25 per day. Imagine if you only had $1.25 to spend for all your living expenses for one day! In wealthier countries, the poor usually have more money but still not enough to meet their needs. Poverty leads to sickness and early death because the poor cannot afford nutritious food needed to stay healthy or health care when they are ill.

Helping others

Poverty in Sub-Saharan Africa is the worst in the world. Extreme poverty affects over 40 percent of the population. An estimated 30,000 children die in Africa every day from poverty and disease. One way to be an anti-poverty activist is to help a humanitarian agency. Humanitarian agencies believe in the value of human life. Through donations, they fund poverty relief work around the world. Ask your teacher about organizing a classroom challenge and get your entire class involved in fundraising. Hold a penny raffle or bake sale and donate the proceeds to a humanitarian agency working in Africa. Do some library research on the causes of poverty. Is there anything you can change in your life that contributes to poverty?

Why does it happen?

Poverty exists because of the unequal division of wealth and goods. In simple terms: some people have a lot and others have very little. The real injustice of poverty is that there is enough wealth in the world to end suffering. The right to a standard of living that meets basic needs such as food, shelter, and health care, is a human right set out by the United Nations. This means that ending poverty requires more than just acts of kindness and charity, such as giving money to the poor. It also requires a commitment to end the inequality that creates poverty.

In wealthier countries, people who are hungry can go to soup kitchens or food banks. These are temporary solutions that keep people from starving, but do not end poverty.

Fighting homelessness

Shelter is a basic human need. Everybody needs a place to live and sleep. Right now, about 100 million people around the world are homeless. Many are poor. They do not have enough money to pay for shelter. Others are on the street because they are mentally ill. Homeless people can be seen on the streets of big cities, but there are other homeless people who are less visible. Homeless families often hide their homelessness by living temporarily with family or friends. These living conditions are stressful and most often do not last.

Discrimination

Homeless people suffer from discrimination. People do not like to see them on the streets or begging. Some people think that the homeless are lazy, but many of them do have jobs. Their jobs just do not pay enough for them to afford to rent or own a home, as well as pay for the cost of food, clothing, and transportation.

Homelessness is often accompanied by poverty and hunger.

20

Fighting homelessness

Homelessness is a human rights issue. The United Nations Declaration of Human Rights states that everyone has the right to a standard of living that is adequate for well being and includes food, clothing, housing, and medical care. For social justice activists, this means that their work is not just about charity, or giving to people in need, but about fighting for people's rights. If having a home is seen as a right, that right must be respected and protected.

It is difficult for homeless people to find places to rest or to wash.

Get Active!

What does it feel like to be homeless?

Think about all the things you do in a day. Imagine doing them without a home and how much harder that would be. You do not have a television, computer, or video games. You do not even have a bed, or a roof over your head. Where do you sleep? What happens when it rains or snows? Where do you go to the bathroom? Where can you take a shower or a bath? How do you keep your clothes clean? How do you carry all of your clothes? How do you keep your personal items if you have no safe place to put them? What about food? Where would you get and keep food? Is there a homeless shelter in your neighborhood? Imagine spending a night there. Now imagine doing this day after day.

Culture of peace

Peace will exist when the world is free from war, violence, oppression, injustice, and inequality. Peace activists believe a peaceful world, or a culture of peace, can only be created through acceptance and understanding.

The way to peace

Mohandas Gandhi, an Indian **pacifist** and activist, famously said, "There is no way to peace; peace is the way." Peace activists believe peaceful actions create a peaceful world. Many social justice activists believe lasting peace can only be achieved when there is no cruel or unjust treatment among people. If a society or a country is oppressed and people are afraid and not free, there is no peace. For social justice activists, fighting injustice becomes the way to peace. This includes addressing human rights abuses and some of the causes of war, or armed conflict.

These young peace activists march to protest a war. Some may also be activists for peace through their consumption habits—by choosing not to buy products produced in a country that is following unjust policies.

Field Notes:

The 14th Dalai Lama is the spiritual and political leader of Tibetan Buddhists. He fled Tibet in 1959, ten years after China invaded the country. Since then, he has lived in India, where he is the leader of a Tibetan government in exile. The Dalai Lama received the **Nobel Peace Prize** in 1989 for his non-violent struggle to free Tibet. He believes peace requires feeling for other people's suffering the way we feel for our own.

The 14th Dalai Lama.

"Peace, in the sense of the absence of war, is of little value to someone who is dying of hunger or cold. It will not remove the pain of torture inflicted on a prisoner of conscience. It does not comfort those who have lost their loved ones in floods caused by senseless deforestation in a neighboring country. Peace can only last where human rights are respected, where the people are fed, and where individuals and nations are free."

Environmental justice

Environmentalists are people who care about and protect Earth — including all the plants, animals, and humans who live on the planet. Some environmentalists are also advocates of social justice. They understand that some people, such as those who live near a toxic waste dump for example, are more threatened by a polluted environment. Environmental justice activists strive to ensure that everyone has the equal right to environmental protection, regardless of their race, income, or culture.

What is environmental justice?

Environmental justice grew from the concerns of civil rights activists that the health of African Americans, Aboriginal peoples, and the poor was more at risk because of the environment they lived in. These people were more likely to have dumps and pollution-creating factories located near their homes. Environmental justice activists believe one way to change was to include people in the decisions that affect them. If a dump was to be located near them, they should have the right to say no to it.

BIG MOUTH

Get Active!

How healthy is your neighborhood?

Environmental justice activists fight for fair treatment, laws, and policies for everyone when it comes to the environment. Is your neighborhood and school healthy? Map them and find out! Are there overflowing trash dumpsters on your way to school? Are there many abandoned buildings? Are there parks nearby? Do they have trees and green areas or are they concrete courts and playgrounds? What about your school? Are there pests (cockroaches or rats) that leave droppings? Is the air inside the school easy to breathe?

The struggle for justice

In 1982, a group of people banded together to oppose a government decision to open a hazardous waste landfill near their homes in Warren County, North Carolina. The landfill accepted soil contaminated with chemicals known to cause cancer. Protests and demonstrations did not prevent the landfill from opening, but they did call attention to the fact that politicians chose to put the dump near a predominantly African-American community. The Warren County protests sparked the environmental justice movement. Today, activists continue the struggle for environmental justice throughout the world.

Factories and dumps are more likely to be in or near low income neighborhoods.

In the trenches

Social justice activists are involved in many causes in different ways. Some are public figures who use their popularity to speak out and encourage change. Others work hands-on in the struggle for social justice.

Graça Machel

An advocate for the rights of women and children, Graça Machel grew up in Mozambique. She later became a government minister in that country, where she worked to improve education and literacy. Machel wrote a 1996 UN report on how children are affected by armed conflict. The report recommended a global campaign to stop children from being recruited as soldiers. Machel was awarded many honors for her years of human rights work. Today, she is a member of the Elders, a group of advocates who try to solve some of the world's problems.

Graça Machel uses her position to influence others to do the right thing.

Ava Lowery

Ava Lowery is a peace activist who began making videos about the Iraq war at age fifteen from her home in Alabama. With two uncles who served in Iraq, Lowery supported the troops but wanted a venue for her opinion that the war was wrong. She set up her own Web site (www.peacetakescourage.com) to post the videos and began researching and writing about peace and politics. Her activism earned her death threats from people who did not agree with her and awards from those who did. Lowery continues to post videos on her Web site, and encourages other young people to connect and get involved through her blog, www.avasarmy.com.

Stephen Lewis

As the United Nations Special Envoy for **HIV/AIDS** in Africa, Stephen Lewis was deeply moved by the struggle of people living with HIV/AIDS and those who cared for them. He was blunt in saying that the world was not doing enough to help fight the disease and keep those with it alive.

Stephen Lewis said it was his job to speak the truth.

Lewis was a politician and diplomat in Canada before serving as the UN Special Envoy. He continues to advocate and support people with HIV/AIDS through the Stephen Lewis Foundation (www.stephenlewisfoundation.org). The foundation funds and provides resources to grassroots organizations in Africa that help women and others living with the disease, and assists orphans and the grandmothers who care for them.

Muhammad Yunus

Muhammad Yunus is an economist and former university professor who established a system and bank for loaning poor people money to start businesses. Yunus established the Grameen Bank in 1976 after seeing the suffering caused by the 1974 famine in his country, Bangladesh. To date, the bank has given out billions in loans – about 94 percent of them to women who have since improved the lives of their families. Yunus and the bank were awarded a Nobel Peace Prize in 2006. The Grameen Bank continues to do what no other bank does: fight poverty by giving people a chance.

What you can do

There are many social justice causes and issues. Activists choose many routes to change. Some pressure governments to make new laws. They do this by writing polite and informed letters to their elected officials. Others volunteer their time to organizations that help people, such as shelters and humanitarian organizations.

Be informed!

Being informed is an important first step in activism. Many activists say they got involved in a cause after being deeply affected by something they saw on television or the Internet. They took the time to learn more by reading books, newspapers, magazines, and Web sites.

Get organized!

Joining together with other people who believe in the same cause is an important way to take action. Start a club at school, a community center, or a place of worship. Get the support of your parents, teachers, school principal, or religious leader. Churches, temples, and mosques are often at the forefront of social justice issues because many religions teach justice and equality. Religious groups may welcome young activists. Speaking to adults about social justice issues calls attention to your cause. Many clubs and social organizations invite public speakers to make presentations. Some may even donate money to a cause if they are persuaded of its importance.

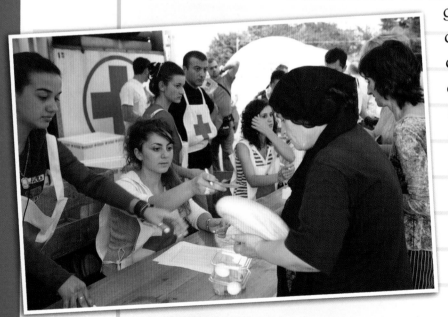

The Red Cross is one organization that needs volunteers.

Write letters

It is easy to write a letter to the editor of a newspaper. Be clear about the issue or cause, get your facts straight, and keep the letter short. Look for the newspaper's address on the editorial page (the page with all the letters.) Follow any directions the newspaper lists for submitting letters to the editor, and mail or email your letter.

The media, such as television, helps bring newsworthy events to a large audience. They are always looking for story ideas.

Get Active!   Write a press release

One way to bring attention to a social justice issue is to write a press release. A press release is a written statement sent to the media (newspapers, radio, and television stations) that brings attention to an issue or cause. The goal is to make the media want to write about the issue, so it should be newsworthy. If you have started a social justice club at your school and you want to hold a rally or sell baked goods to raise funds, write a press release telling the media of your plans. Give the media all the information needed, including how the club formed and why. Include dates and times for events and a contact person and phone number. This means you must also get an adult involved, such as a parent or teacher. Make sure you have approval for what you are doing.

LATEST NEWS

Social justice groups

On this page, you will find Web sites of some well-known organizations that appear in this book. It is important that you view these sites with your teacher or parent. Some Web sites or links from these sites may contain topics and images of a sensitive nature. Discuss the information you read on these Web sites with your teacher or parent, and then make up your own mind about how you feel about the subject.

Doctors Without Borders

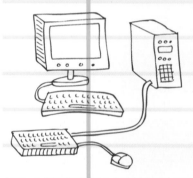

Doctors Without Borders is an independent humanitarian organization that provides medical aid to people whose lives are threatened by armed conflicts, diseases, and disasters. It operates in 60 countries throughout the world, and its volunteers speak out about human rights abuses. The group's Web site contains information on its work and how donations help. Visit www.doctorswithoutborders.org.

Panos

Panos is an international development agency that believes that poor and marginalized people should be able to determine the changes needed to improve their lives. Panos works with independent institutes in eight countries on research and projects such as building peace and fighting discrimination. The Panos Web site can be used as a source for information on social justice issues. Its Web address is: www.panos.org.uk.

Oxfam

Oxfam is an international relief and development agency
that operates in more than 100 countries.
Visit Oxfam at www.oxfam.org.

Care

Care is an agency that fights global poverty and provides
emergency aid. See Care's Web site at: www.care.org.

Free the Children

Free the Children is an international children's rights
organization that focuses on ending child poverty and
exploitation. The organization's Web site is an excellent
place to find information on becoming a youth activist.
Check it out at: www.freethechildren.com.

Global Exchange

Global Exchange is a social justice education organization.
Its Web site is: www.globalexchange.org.

GET ACTIVE!

Glossary

advocate A person who publicly supports a cause

agitate To stir up public feelings and discussions

civil rights The rights of citizens to political and social freedoms

democracy A system of government where representatives are elected by the people

devalue To underestimate the importance of someone or something

developing world Areas of the world that are seeking to become more economically and socially advanced

diversity Something that shows a great deal of variety or difference

entitled Something someone has a right to

environmentalist A person who is concerned about and protects the environment

ethical Something that is principled or right

gender The cultural or social state of being male or female

grassroots The most basic level of organized activity

HIV/AIDS Human Immunodeficiency Virus is the virus that causes Acquired Immune Deficiency Syndrome, a disease that lowers a person's resistance to other killer diseases

humanitarian agency An organization that seeks to help people and promote human welfare

marginalized To make insignificant or unimportant

Nobel Peace Prize A prize awarded each year to people for their outstanding work for peace

nutritious Food that is healthful

oppressed To keep someone in subservience or hardship

pacifist Someone who believes that any violence, including war, is unjust

prejudice A preconceived notion not based on reason or fact

refugee Someone who has been forced to leave their country to escape war, persecution, or a natural disaster

repression To subdue someone or something by force

social inequality When individuals in a society do not have equal status, or equal rights and freedoms, such as the right to vote or freedom of speech

suffragette A woman who advocates for a woman's right to vote

United Nations An international organization of countries established in 1945 to promote peace, security, and cooperation

violate To treat disrespectfully; to disregard

vulnerable Liable to be harmed or attacked

Index

Printed in China — CT